ANCIENT GREECE

BUILDERS, TRADERS & CRAFTSMEN

JANE SHUTER

Heinemann
LIBRARY

First published in Great Britain by Heinemann Library
Halley Court, Jordan Hill, Oxford OX2 8EJ
a division of Reed Educational and Professional Publishing Ltd.
Heinemann is a registered trademark of Reed Educational & Professional Publishing Limited.

OXFORD MELBOURNE AUCKLAND KUALA LUMPUR
SINGAPORE IBADAN NAIROBI KAMPALA JOHANNESBURG
GABORONE PORTSMOUTH NH CHICAGO

Designed by Celia Floyd
Illustrations by Jeff Edwards and Donald Harley
Printed in Hong Kong by Wing King Tong Co., Ltd.

02 01 00 99
10 9 8 7 6 5 4 3 2

ISBN 0 431 00500 1

British Library Cataloguing in Publication Data

Shuter, Jane
   Greece : builders, traders and craftsmen. - (Ancient world topic books)
   1 . Architecture, Greek - Juvenile literature 2 . Greece - Commerce - Juvenile Literature 3 . Greece - History - To 146 B. C. - Juvenile literature
   I . Title
   938

Acknowledgements
The Publishers would like to thank the following for permission to reproduce photographs:
Alinari-Giraudon p21; Ancient Art and Architecture Collection pp5, 7; Ashmolean Museum p23; British Museum pp20, 28; C M Dixon p22; Hirmer Fotoarchiv p19; Metropolitan Museum of Art, New York pp17, 26; Royal Ontario Museum p 11.

Cover photograph reproduced with permission of the Ashmolean Museum

Any words appearing in the text in bold, **like this**, are explained in the Glossary.

CONTENTS

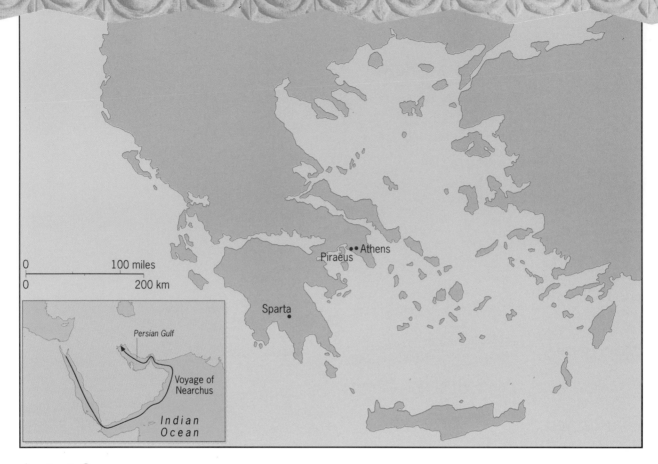

Ancient Greece

BUILDERS

Ancient Greek builders made **temples** and huge statues out of stone with very simple tools. They built ordinary houses with mud bricks. Few houses have survived for us to look at now. They have crumbled away or been built over.

Timeline

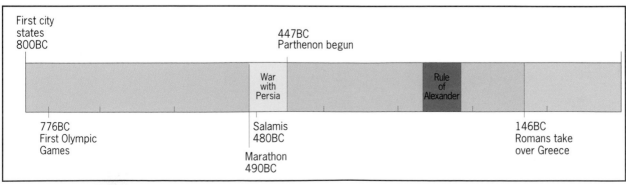

First city states 800BC

447BC Parthenon begun

War with Persia

Rule of Alexander

776BC First Olympic Games

Salamis 480BC

146BC Romans take over Greece

Marathon 490BC

CRAFTSMEN AND TRADERS

Some Ancient Greek cities, especially Athens, were large. There were many **craftsmen** living in the cities, making things like pots, statues, boots and vases. Some **goods** that craftsmen made, especially the beautifully decorated pottery, were in great demand in other countries.

Merchants were important, too. They traded goods from the **city states** for things that the **citizens** needed. They usually needed foods, like **grain** for bread. They traded with other city states and with Greek **colonies** in other countries.

Many modern buildings, like the British Museum shown here, copy the building styles of the Ancient Greeks.

Builders used stone to build the most important buildings in a city. They used stone for **temples** and theatres. They also used stone for the public baths and the buildings around the main square, known as the **agora**.

BUILDING TOOLS

Builders did not have machines to dig and flatten the ground or lift things. They needed lots of workers. They used pulleys and ropes to lift things. Most of the heavy work, such as hauling stone around, was done by **slaves**. Aristotle, a Greek thinker, called slaves 'a tool that just happens to be alive'.

BUILDING RULES

The Ancient Greeks thought things were more beautiful if they looked balanced. So the best kind of temple was a rectangle with matching porches front and back, and the same number of columns along each side. Its length, width, the width of the columns and the spaces between them all had to have the same **mathematical ratio**.

The Parthenon, Athens. The building was begun in 447BC and was finished in 432BC. The carving and decoration took six years to complete.

BUILDING THE PARTHENON

The Parthenon is a huge **temple** built to honour the goddess Athena. It was built between 447 and 432BC. It was built almost entirely with **marble**. This was very heavy, expensive and hard to move. Blocks were cut to size at the **quarries**. The temple is covered with carvings showing scenes from stories about the lives of the gods.

THE COST

The Parthenon cost a lot to build. It cost about 12,000,000 drachmae. A builder could earn a drachma a day, a sailor could earn half a drachma. A **slave** cost about 100 drachmae.

A GREEK WRITER DESCRIBED SOME OF THE PEOPLE WHO WORKED ON THE PARTHENON:

Carpenters, modellers, coppersmiths, dyers, stonemasons, workers in gold and ivory, painters, embroiderers and engravers. Also carriers and suppliers of materials — **merchants**, sailors, wagon-makers, drivers. Also rope-makers, weavers, leather workers, road builders, miners. Each craft also had its own group of labourers to fetch and carry.

Building the Parthenon.

The Ancient Greeks decorated their **temples** and public buildings with stone carvings. They also made beautiful statues, mostly from **marble** or **bronze**. At the centre of the Parthenon was a statue of the goddess Athena, about ten metres tall. It was made by Phidias, who was famous for his huge statues. First, Phidias made a wooden frame exactly the right shape. Athena's face, arms and feet were made from carefully carved ivory. Her eyes were made from precious stones. Her long dress, helmet and shield were made of gold. They were all carefully fitted on to the frame.

PHIDIAS – A THIEF?

Phidias' enemies accused him of keeping some of the gold from the statue. Luckily, he had made the pieces of gold removable. He took the statue apart and weighed the pieces in public to show he was not a thief. Then someone pointed out that Phidias had put himself and Pericles, an important man in Athens, in the picture of a battle on the statue's shield. He was accused of not showing the goddess enough respect. He left the city and went to work somewhere else.

This is what Phidias' statue of Athena probably looked like. It is a modern reconstruction in a museum.

Important Greek buildings were made from stone. What about ordinary workshops and homes? These were made from mud bricks on a stone base. The bricks were so crumbly that burglars were called 'wall piercers'.

It is very hard to tell what an ordinary street in Athens looked like. A visitor at the time described the streets as narrow and winding, and the buildings as old and needing repair. But there are no better descriptions. Homes in Athens have crumbled away and been built over many times. There are some abandoned towns in other parts of Greece where the stone bases of houses remain. These buildings give us clues about Athens.

HOUSES

Most Ancient Greek houses were built around a courtyard. The windows and doors were small. Each home had a part of the house for the women and a more public part for the men. The most important room in the house, the **andron** (where men ate and gave parties) sometimes had a tiled floor. The other floors were made of beaten earth.

A residential
street in Athens.

Piraeus was the **port** of Athens from 493BC onwards. As Athens became more important, Piraeus became a town itself. There was a paved road that ran the 6.2 kilometres from Athens to Piraeus, with high walls each side to keep the road safe.

WHAT WENT ON IN PIRAEUS?

The Athenian **navy** kept their ships at Piraeus. It was also a big **trade** port. It had docks for ships and warehouses for the **merchants**. It had meeting places, shops, workshops, **temples** and theatres. It had grand public baths with a big bath deep enough for several people to jump into — most public baths had small baths people sat in to scoop water over themselves.

NOT ALWAYS GUARDED

The walls between Athens and Piraeus, and the walls around Piraeus, were pulled down in 404BC, when the Spartans won a war against Athens. Spartan generals watched the walls come down, while girls played music on flutes to celebrate. The walls were rebuilt in 393BC, when Athens was strong.

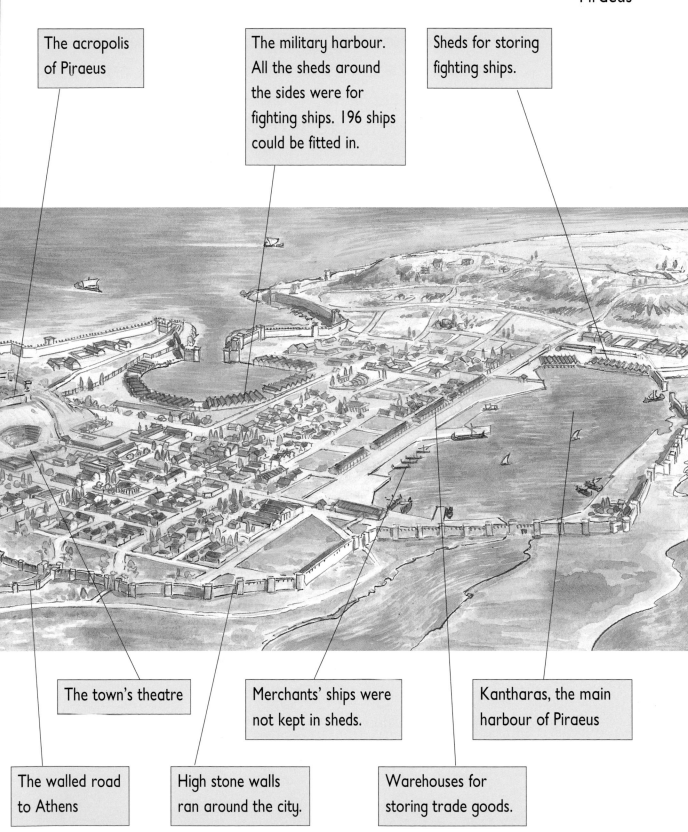

The acropolis of Piraeus

The military harbour. All the sheds around the sides were for fighting ships. 196 ships could be fitted in.

Sheds for storing fighting ships.

The town's theatre

Merchants' ships were not kept in sheds.

Kantharas, the main harbour of Piraeus

The walled road to Athens

High stone walls ran around the city.

Warehouses for storing trade goods.

TRADE

Trade was very important to the Greek **city states**. They did not grow enough food to feed everyone, so they had to trade to get food. City states also traded to get **goods** like tin (which they needed but could not be mined in Greece) and luxury goods such as silk cloth and glass bowls. They traded with other city states, with other countries and with **colonies**.

Places where various Greek city states traded.

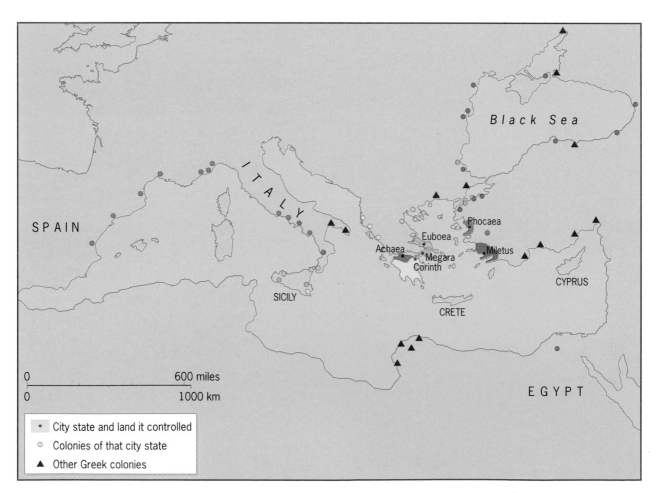

WHAT DID THEY TRADE?

The Greek city states all made enough wine and olive oil to trade. Some city states were also famous for other things. Miletus made very soft, fine woollen cloth. Athens made pottery decorated with black and red scenes from stories about the gods and everyday life. Greek traders traded different things at different places, depending on what those places needed and what they had to spare.

These **merchants** are weighing goods on a large balance scale.

TRADING WITH EGYPT

Greece had a lot of silver in the ground that could be mined. Egypt had very little silver, but most years it had more **grain** than it needed. These things made a good trade. They were not the only things Greece and Egypt traded. Egypt traded carved ivory and linen cloth for Greek **slaves** or olive oil.

Merchants could make a lot of money by trading, but they took risks too. Merchants often lost ships full of **goods** in bad weather. The writer Hesiod warned; 'Go to sea, if you must, only from June to September – and even then you are a fool to go!'

CHEATING THE BANK IN 360BC

Not all shipwrecks were due to bad weather. Many merchants borrowed money to **trade**. Banks often agreed that if the ship sank they would not ask for their money back. Some merchants tried to cheat the banks.

Hegestratos, a ship owner, and his agent, Zenothemis, signed a document saying a ship was loaded with **grain** for Athens. In fact, it was empty. About two days from land Hegestratos made a hole in the ship and leapt overboard. But he could not find his small escape boat in the darkness and drowned. Zenothemis tried to get everyone to leave the ship, saying it would sink. But they stayed on board and got the ship to land. People could see that it was empty and that they had tried to cheat. We know about this because the bank took Zenothemis to court, and the story was written down.

This pot shows how important trade could be to a country. The ruler of Cyrene (a Greek colony in North Africa) is supervising the packing.

JUST ONE TRADING SHIP

Archaeologists found the wreck of a trading ship near Cyprus, dating from about 350BC. They worked out that the ship was about 15 metres long and had one sail. It was carrying wine (from Rhodes), millstones for grinding corn (from Kos) and almonds (from Cyprus).

The weather was not the only danger for trading ships. Pirates were a danger too. Their ships were faster than trading ships, which were built to carry a lot of cargo, not for speed.

This vase painting shows pirates attacking a trading ship.

Piracy was not seen as a bad thing, and was a way of life for many people, as long as they obeyed the rules! These included not raiding ships from countries or **city states** that were friendly with their own part of Greece.

FISHERMEN

Pirates and traders had bigger ships, but most of the ships at sea were fishing boats. Fishermen had small, shallow boats that could move easily round rocky shores and islands. They fished with nets, and also caught lobsters in wicker pots.

A carving of the goddess Athena helping the adventurer Jason get ready for a voyage.

EXPLORING OTHER SEAS

The Ancient Greeks were careful sailors. They sailed by day, landed at night and always tried to keep land in sight. They did explore, looking for new places to settle in and **trade** with.

NEARCHUS

Alexander (356–323BC) was the first ruler to lead many **city states**. In 325BC he sent a captain, called Nearchus, with about 1000 ships to explore the Indian Ocean. The huge waves were a shock because they were used to the calmer Mediterranean Sea. The men were very seasick! They sailed to the Persian Gulf, digging through sand bars and landing to find food. They often had to fight for it! At last, they reached the Persian Gulf. Alexander was glad to see them – he feared they had drowned. A Greek historian, writing later, said: 'Their hair was long and neglected, their bodies filthy and shrivelled.'

Greek cities all had **craftsmen** who made different things. In some cities, especially Athens, there were many different crafts. Most craftsmen worked in small workshops of between ten and thirty workers. People who made the same things often had workshops in the same part of the city. A craftsman earned about one drachma a day. This was twice as much as an ordinary workman, who earned only enough to live on.

IN ABOUT 414BC ARISTOPHANES, A GREEK WRITER, DESCRIBED THE BUSTLE OF A MORNING IN ATHENS:

When the cock crows at dawn, up they all jump and rush off to work, the **bronze**-smiths, the potters, the tanners, the shoemakers, the bath attendants, the corn merchants, the lyre-makers, the shield-makers. Some of them even put on their sandals and go when it is still dark.

A gold necklace from a craft workshop.

SMALLER CITIES

Smaller cities did not have such a wide range of craftsmen as Athens. There were not as many people and they were not as rich. So they bought less expensive luxuries and lived more simply. A craftsman had to do many different jobs to make a living.

This shoemaker is cutting out a child's shoe. His tools are on the wall at the back. He has water in a large bowl because wet leather is easier to cut.

IN ABOUT 300BC THE GREEK WRITER XENOPHON DESCRIBED THE GOOD THING ABOUT PEOPLE HAVING SPECIAL SKILLS.

In small city states the same man makes beds, doors, ploughs, tables, even builds houses too. It is impossible for a man who works at so many crafts to be very good at all of them. In a big **city state** there are enough people for a man to make a living from one craft. In some places one man cuts shoes, another stitches them up.

Pottery containers were important for storing food, oil and drink. People ate from pottery plates and dishes. They drank from pottery bowls and cups. Even small villages needed a potter to make everyday things. Most pottery was quite plain. But the most famous Greek pottery is the decorated pottery, mainly from Athens. Museums today have more of this type of pottery on show because it is so beautiful, but potters would have made more of the plain type.

ATHENIAN POTTERY

The Potters' District of Athens was near the river. The clay the potters used had a lot of iron in it, so once baked it became a reddish colour. Athenian vase painters used black as a contrasting colour. They painted detailed scenes of everyday life and also scenes from stories of the time about gods, goddesses and heroes.

Historians think the smaller cups and dishes cost between one and two drachmae, the bigger pots and vases between two and three. Really well made and decorated pots could have cost more.